YOUR PASSPORT TO

BRAZIL

by Nancy Dickmann

CAPSTONE PRESS
a capstone imprint

Published by Capstone Press, an imprint of Capstone
1710 Roe Crest Drive, North Mankato, Minnesota 56003
capstonepub.com

Library of Congress Cataloging-in-Publication Data is available on the Library
of Congress website.
ISBN: 9781666389975 (hardcover)
ISBN: 9781666389920 (paperback)
ISBN: 9781666389937 (ebook PDF)

Summary: What is it like to live in or visit Brazil? What makes Brazil's culture
unique? Explore the geography, traditions, and daily lives of Brazilians.

Editorial Credits
Editor: Carrie Sheely; Designer: Elyse White; Media Researcher: Jo Miller;
Production Specialist: Tori Abraham

Image Credits
Alamy: Pulsar Imagens, 19, REUTERS, 27; Capstone Press: Eric Gohl, 5; Getty
Images: DANIEL RAMALHO, 25; Shutterstock: Alexandre Rotenberg, 29, Alf
Ribeiro, 9, 11, Cassiohabib, 28, Catarina Belova, 17, Celso Pupo, 24, cifotart,
16, Felipecbit, 12, IrenaV, cover (bottom), m2art, cover (map), Nelson Antoine,
7, 23, Ondrej Prosicky, 13, 15, Paulo Vilela, 20, RedlineVector, cover (flag),
worldclassphoto, 14

Design Elements
iStockphoto, Shutterstock Images

All internet sites appearing in back matter were available and accurate when
this book was sent to press.

CONTENTS

Words in **bold** are in the glossary.

CHAPTER ONE

WELCOME TO BRAZIL!

The sun is shining. Ocean waves lap at the shore. Some people play soccer or volleyball on the golden sand. Food sellers walk up and down the beach, offering tasty snacks. This is the beautiful Copacabana Beach. It is more than 2 miles (3.2 kilometers) long. It is part of Rio de Janeiro on the coast of Brazil.

Brazil is the biggest country in South America. More than 200 million people live in Brazil. It is a land of great natural beauty. It is also home to many **cultures**.

MAP OF BRAZIL

Amazon River

Manaus

BRAZIL

BRASÍLIA

Pantanal

Rio de Janeiro

São Paulo

Christ the Redeemer statue

Iguaçu Falls

- ■ Capital City
- ● City
- ⬡ Landform
- △ Landmarks
- ■ Amazon Rain Forest

Explore Brazil's cities and landmarks.

FACT FILE

OFFICIAL NAME: FEDERATIVE REPUBLIC OF BRAZIL
POPULATION: 214,891,000
LAND AREA: 3,227,096 SQ. MI. (8,358,140 SQ KM)
CAPITAL: BRASÍLIA
MONEY: BRAZILIAN REAL
GOVERNMENT: FEDERAL PRESIDENTIAL REPUBLIC
LANGUAGE: PORTUGUESE (OFFICIAL) AND OTHERS, INCLUDING INDIGENOUS LANGUAGES

GEOGRAPHY: Brazil is in eastern South America. The Atlantic Ocean forms its east coast. It has borders with all but two of the other South American countries.

NATURAL RESOURCES: Brazil has oil, iron ore, rubber, and gemstones. Farmers raise livestock and grow soybeans, sugarcane, corn, and coffee.

ONE NATION, MANY CULTURES

Modern Brazil is a mix of different cultures. Explorers from Portugal arrived in the 1500s. Some of these explorers stayed. Later, people were brought to Brazil from Africa. They were enslaved and forced to do work.

Today, almost half of Brazilians are mixed race. Nearly everyone speaks Portuguese.

Indigenous people dance and sing during a demonstration in São Paulo, Brazil.

INDIGENOUS PEOPLE

Many **Indigenous** people live in Brazil. Most of them are in the northern areas. They live off the land in the Amazon **Rain Forest**. They still speak their own languages. They protect their traditions and way of life. Much of their land has been stolen. Other people want to use it for farming or mining. Some groups have had no contact with the outside world.

CHAPTER TWO

HISTORY OF BRAZIL

The first people in Brazil hunted and gathered food to eat. Later, some began farming. By the time European explorers arrived, several million people lived in Brazil. The biggest groups spoke a language called Tupian.

EUROPEANS ARRIVE

Pedro Álvares Cabral arrived in Brazil in 1500. He claimed the land for Portugal. Other explorers came after him. Many came from Portugal. Others came from France and the Netherlands. Some people who came to Brazil set up huge farms. They grew sugarcane. They enslaved Indigenous people to work in the fields. They also kidnapped people from Africa and enslaved them.

A statue of Pedro Álvares Cabral stands in front of Ibirapuera Park in São Paulo, Brazil.

FACT

Early Portuguese explorers called Brazil "Land of the Holy Cross." Traders soon came to harvest the brazilwood trees that grew there. They called it "land of brazil" because of the trees. The name stuck.

TIMELINE OF BRAZILIAN HISTORY

ABOUT 9000 BCE: Indigenous people live in Brazil.

1500 CE: The first European explorers reach Brazil. Pedro Álvares Cabral claims it for Portugal.

1822: Brazil declares its independence. Pedro I becomes the first emperor of Brazil.

1831: Pedro II becomes the emperor.

1888: Slavery is outlawed in Brazil.

1889: Brazil becomes a republic.

1942–1945: Brazil fights in World War II on the side of the Allies.

1960: The capital moves from Rio de Janeiro to Brasília.

2010: Dilma Rousseff is elected the country's first female president.

2016: Brazil becomes the first South American country to host the Olympic Games.

INDEPENDENT COUNTRY

Some Brazilians didn't want to be ruled by Portugal. They wanted to make their own laws. In 1822, they declared their **independence**. Pedro I became the first leader of the Empire of Brazil. His son, Pedro II, became emperor in 1831. He was only 5 years old. Other government leaders made decisions until Pedro II was 14. He became a very popular ruler.

Today, machines help workers harvest coffee in Brazil.

The country's population grew. So did the **economy**. Brazilians sold crops, such as coffee beans and sugar, around the world. Pedro II made slavery illegal in 1888.

In 1889, Brazil became a republic. Under the new government, the states had more power than they once did.

CHAPTER THREE

EXPLORE BRAZIL

Brazil is a huge country. It has different landforms. There are mountains and steep cliffs. There are rolling hills, huge **plains**, and rushing rivers. Offshore islands have beautiful beaches and amazing wildlife. The Amazon Rain Forest covers a large area in the north. Most of the country has a tropical climate. It stays warm all year.

Visitors to Chapada dos Guimarães National Park can see hills and cliffs.

Caimans lie by a river in the Pantanal.

WONDERFUL WETLANDS

Parts of Brazil have dry grasslands. But one of the country's most amazing landscapes is a wetland. The Pantanal is in west-central Brazil. It is one of the world's largest wetlands. Each year it floods, forming shallow lakes and marshes. Many animals live there. Caimans lie in the shallow waters. Bright macaws fly overhead.

FACT

The Iguaçu Falls are on the border between Brazil and Argentina. The horseshoe-shaped falls are nearly 2 miles (3.2 kilometers) wide!

The Amazon River is one of the longest rivers in the world.

IN THE AMAZON RAIN FOREST

The Amazon Rain Forest is the world's largest rain forest. It covers an area nearly eight times the size of Texas. About 60 percent of the rain forest is in Brazil. The mighty Amazon River runs through it. This river flows from the Andes Mountains to the Atlantic Ocean. Smaller rivers link up with the Amazon.

PLANTS AND ANIMALS

The Amazon Rain Forest is an important **ecosystem**. Many plants and animals live there. Some of them are found nowhere else on Earth. Tall trees form a canopy. Monkeys, birds, and tree frogs live in their branches. There are smaller shrubs and trees below. Tortoises and anteaters look for food in the shade.

Anteaters use their long snouts to pick up the scent of ants.

SHRINKING FOREST

People are cutting down parts of the rain forest. They want to use trees for wood. They clear land for farming and ranching. This is called deforestation. A large area is lost every year. Some groups are working to protect the Amazon.

BUSY CITIES

Rio de Janeiro is one of Brazil's most famous cities. It was the capital until 1960. Rio de Janeiro is on Brazil's southeastern coast. Tourists stroll along the beautiful beaches. They enjoy live music and samba dancing. Some tourists go to see the enormous statue of Jesus that looks down over Rio de Janeiro from a mountaintop.

São Paulo is Brazil's largest city. It is known for its banking, manufacturing, and technology industries.

Brasília is known for its buildings. Some of them look like sculptures.

FACT

Batman's Alley is a narrow street in São Paulo. The walls on each side are covered in graffiti art. Artists from all over paint here. The pictures are always changing.

São Paulo has many modern skyscrapers.

Beachgoers enjoy Copacabana Beach in Rio de Janeiro.

RAIN FOREST CITY

Most people in Brazil live on the coast. Manaus is an inland city in the Amazon Rain Forest. It is an important port. Long ago, harvesting rubber made this city rich. Today, tourists visit its beautiful opera house.

CHAPTER FOUR

DAILY LIFE

Family is important to Brazilians. Extended families often live near one another. In the cities, life is fast-paced and busy. In rural areas, it is much quieter.

There is a large wealth gap in Brazil. The rich live in fancy homes. Many poor Brazilians live in **favelas**. These neighborhoods have grown at the edges of Rio de Janeiro and other big cities. Most homes in favelas are simple and squashed close together.

SCHOOL

Most children in Brazil go to school. However, nearly half stop by the age of 15. This happens most often in poor or rural areas. Most schools divide the day into two or three "shifts." They last four or five hours. Each student attends only one shift.

Schoolchildren attend class in Varzea Funda.

A bowl of feijoada
with side dishes

FOOD

Brazilians love sharing meals. Long lunches are a time to chat with friends. Dinners are a time to spend with family. Food in Brazil is a mix of the country's different cultures. The national dish is a stew called feijoada. It is made of pork, sausage, and black beans.

Many Brazilian dishes include manioc. This root comes from the Amazon Rain Forest. It can be boiled or made into fries. People use ground manioc flour to make bread.

Brazilians enjoy eating grilled meat, especially beef. They put it on long skewers to cook.

BRIGADEIROS

These bite-size chocolate treats are often served at parties. Their name means "general." They were invented as part of a political campaign when an army general ran for president.

Brigadeiros Ingredients:
- 3 tablespoons unsalted butter
- 1 14-ounce can sweetened condensed milk
- pinch of salt
- 4 tablespoons cocoa powder
- 1 teaspoon vanilla
- toppings such as chopped nuts, sprinkles, or shredded coconut
- mini paper baking cups

Brigadeiros Directions:

1. In a pan, heat the butter and condensed milk with the cocoa and a pinch of salt.
2. Stir the mixture until it boils, then reduce the heat.
3. Keep stirring as you cook the mixture for another 10–15 minutes. It is ready when it looks thick and shiny and pulls away from the bottom of the pan.
4. Add the vanilla and stir.
5. Put the mixture on a greased plate and chill for at least 2 hours.
6. Roll the mixture into walnut-sized balls, then roll them in your chosen topping to coat the outside. Place each one in a mini paper baking cup to serve.

CHAPTER FIVE
HOLIDAYS AND CELEBRATIONS

Most Brazilians are Christian. Christian holidays and festivals are celebrated around the country. Christmas happens during Brazil's summer. Most people choose a plastic tree to decorate. The main celebration is on Christmas Eve. Families get together for food and music. They count down to midnight.

On January 6, many Brazilians hold festivities for Three Kings Day. They celebrate the Three Wise Men visiting baby Jesus.

FACT

On October 12, some Brazilians celebrate Our Lady of Aparecida Day. People go to visit the Basilica of Our Lady of Aparecida in Brazil. The day is a holiday. People also celebrate Children's Day on October 12.

CARNIVAL

Brazil's most famous festival is Carnival. Lent is the period leading up to Easter. Before it starts, there is a huge party. People dress in fancy costumes. There are parades of samba dancers. Drummers and other musicians march alongside the floats. Carnival takes place across Brazil. The party in Rio de Janeiro is the biggest.

People play instruments to celebrate Carnival.

OTHER HOLIDAYS

Brazilians celebrate their independence from Portugal on September 7. There are military parades, air shows, and fireworks. People fly flags and wave banners. They often gather for picnics.

In June, a folklore festival takes place in the Amazon region. It is a contest between two teams. The teams use music and dance to retell an old legend about an ox. The best team wins.

Many cities hold parades in Brazil to celebrate Independence Day.

Women go into the ocean to jump waves on New Year's Eve in 2019.

NEW YEAR TRADITIONS

On New Year's Eve, many Brazilians go to the beach. They jump over seven waves to bring good luck. People wear white clothes.

On New Year's Day, many people celebrate Iemanjá. She is the goddess of the sea in the candomblé religion. This religion mixes Christianity with other beliefs. At the shore, people put flowers into the water. These are gifts for the goddess.

CHAPTER SIX

SPORTS AND RECREATION

Many Brazilians love soccer. It is the country's most popular sport. Children and adults play it on streets and beaches. Fans follow their favorite pro teams. The Brazilian national teams are very good. The men's team has won the World Cup several times.

Volleyball is also popular in Brazil. Brazilian teams often win world tournaments. Many people play it for fun. They play on indoor courts and on beaches.

Some Brazilians also play footvolley. This sport was invented in Brazil and combines soccer with volleyball. The rules are similar to beach volleyball, but players are not allowed to use their hands.

Neymar da Silva Santos Jr. is a star soccer player for the men's Brazil national team.

LUTA DE GALO

People used to watch rooster fights in Brazil. They were outlawed long ago, but this popular children's game imitates those fights.

1. Two people play against each other. Each "fighter" tucks a scarf or bandanna into their waistband.
2. They cross their right arm across their chest. This arm cannot be used. (If a player is left-handed, they should cross their left arm instead.)
3. When the "fight" begins, the players hop on one leg. They try to grab the other player's scarf with their free hand.
4. Whoever grabs the other's scarf wins. However, if a player puts their foot down or unfolds their arm, they lose.

Many people learn capoeira for fun and exercise.

DANCE AND MUSIC

Music and dancing are a big part of Brazilian culture. In the 1950s, musicians in Brazil made a

A band plays bossa nova on Copacabana Beach.

new type of music. They blended samba with cool jazz. They called it bossa nova. Folk music is also performed around the country. In the northeast, people sing in poetry contests. They make up the words as they go.

Capoeira is a sport that looks like a dance. This **martial art** was invented by enslaved people from Africa. The moves are graceful and dance-like. Drummers tap out a beat. Capoeira was a way of secretly learning to fight.

SOMETHING FOR EVERYONE

Brazil is an amazing country, full of life and energy. Brazilian people are known for being friendly and welcoming. From beaches to rain forests, there is something for everyone to enjoy.

GLOSSARY

culture (KUHL-chuhr)
a people's way of life, ideas, art, customs, and traditions

economy (ee-KON-uh-mee)
the way a country produces, distributes, and uses its money, goods, natural resources, and services

ecosystem (EE-koh-sis-tuhm)
a group of animals and plants that work together with their surroundings

favela (fuh-VE-luh)
a settlement of shacks on the outskirts of a Brazilian city

independence (in-di-PEN-duhnss)
the state of not being ruled or controlled by another country

Indigenous (in-DIH-jen-us)
a way to describe the first people who lived in a certain area

martial art (MAR-shul ART)
styles of self-defense and fighting; tae kwon do, judo, and karate are examples of martial arts

plain (PLAYN)
a large, flat area of land with few trees

rain forest (RAYN FOR-ist)
a thick forest or jungle where at least 100 inches (254 centimeters) of rain falls every year

READ MORE

Esquivel, Gloria Susana. *South America*. New York: Children's Press, 2019.

Juarez, Christine. *South America: A 4D Book*. North Mankato, MN: Capstone, 2019.

Silen, Andrea. *Rainforests*. Washington, D.C.: National Geographic Kids, 2020.

INTERNET SITES

Britannica Kids: Brazil
kids.britannica.com/kids/article/Brazil/345654

DK Findout!: Amazon Rainforest
dkfindout.com/uk/animals-and-nature/habitats-and-ecosystems/amazon-rainforest/

National Geographic Kids:
Discover This Super-Cool Country!
natgeokids.com/uk/discover/geography/countries/country-fact-file-brazil/

INDEX

ABOUT THE AUTHOR

Nancy Dickmann grew up reading encyclopedias for fun, and after many years working in children's publishing, she now has her dream job as a full-time author. She has had over 200 titles published so far, mainly on science topics, and finds that the best part of the job is researching and learning new things. One highlight was getting to interview a real astronaut about using the toilet in space!

SELECT BOOKS IN THIS SERIES

YOUR PASSPORT TO AUSTRALIA   YOUR PASSPORT TO GERMANY
YOUR PASSPORT TO BRAZIL   YOUR PASSPORT TO JAPAN
YOUR PASSPORT TO EGYPT   YOUR PASSPORT TO MEXICO
YOUR PASSPORT TO ENGLAND   YOUR PASSPORT TO SOUTH AFRICA